The Supernatural Kids Cookbook

To Vedra, my number one recipe tester.

The Supernatural Kids Cookbook - Haile's Favorites

Copyright © 2013 by Nancy Mehagian and Huqua Press

ISBN 978-0-9838120-6-7

Library of Congress Control Number: 2013951068

First published in 2013 by Huqua Press
A division of Magpye Media/Morling Manor Corp.
Los Angeles, California

Art Direction by Alexandra Conn

HUQUA PRESS
huquapress.com

Printed in the United States of America.

The Supernatural Kids Cookbook supports the efforts of the Share Our Strength/No Kid Hungry
effort to end childhood hunger.
Take the pledge at NoKidHungry.org

The Supernatural Kids Cookbook

by Nancy Mehagian
with Haile Thomas

illustrations by Alexandra Conn

"Haile's energy and enthusiasm for educating others on how to live healthy is contagious."

– Chelsea Clinton

I am so excited to share my fifty favorite **Supernatural Kids Recipes** and all the reasons why I love them so much. I admire Nancy Mehagian's passion for healthy food and I appreciate that her recipes are foods kids can prepare and the whole family can enjoy. I've included five of my own super YUMMY creations as well and I hope that you will enjoy making and eating all these recipes as much as I do.

My *love* for cooking began when I was five years old. I remember having so much fun helping my mom in the kitchen, and by the time I was nine years old, I was creating meals on my own. The kitchen is my science lab, and I am not afraid to experiment in it! I also believe that learning to **cook** is a great stepping-stone to making other healthy lifestyle choices. Cooking has made me interested in learning more about where my ingredients come from, how nutritious they are, and definitely how to make them *TASTE* amazing. It's a great feeling knowing that what I EAT will nourish my body and help me to do well in school and in my favorite fun physical activities.

Don't be afraid of the kitchen. After all, these recipes were created for us! I know you will enjoy them and be inspired to concoct your own supernatural, healthy, and tasty creations for you and your family.

Haile Thomas

p.s. Look for my notes on Nancy's awesome recipes
in this color ink throughout the cookbook.

TABLE OF CONTENTS

SALADS

Main Dishes

Cakes, Cookies & Desserts

Extras

INTRODUCTION

When I was a **kid**, one of my jobs was to help my mom in the kitchen. I wasn't crazy about setting the table, but loved it when she let me chop and dice the ingredients for her party appetizers or when she let me mix up pancake batter and form fun shapes on the griddle. I also loved BAKING COOKIES for my older brother's *friends* and getting compliments afterwards. For me, cooking has always been an adventure, just like it is for my friend Haile, who discovered her *passion* for healthy cooking at a really young age and has been INSPIRING kids all over the country ever since.

One of my biggest *adventures* was opening the first vegetarian health food restaurant in Spain on a beautiful island called Ibiza. I have been conjuring up delicious and **healthy** foods ever since. I've traveled the world and have never been afraid to sample new foods and cultures. And some of the great **recipes** I found in my travels are here in this book.

Haile and I both love to experiment in the kitchen, cooking for family and friends, and we both love to teach kids the MAGIC of taking a handful of ingredients and turning them into something special and delicious. Cooking can be a lot more **fun** than texting or playing video games. I hope you'll discover for yourself the adventures that are waiting for you in the kitchen and that your belly will be doing a happy dance as you feed it with the food you have lovingly prepared. You're on your way to becoming a **Supernatural Kid** and Junior Chef.

— Nancy Mehagian

The Supernatural Kids Cookbook

A good chef cooks from the heart.

BEFORE YOU BEGIN...

Before You Begin...

Wash your hands with soap and warm water. (Get off to a clean start!)

Have some kitchen towels handy and wear an *apron*.

Read each recipe all the way through and make sure you understand all the steps. Sometimes directions are also found in the list of `ingredients`. For example, a recipe may state: egg, slightly beaten. This means you should lightly beat the egg before adding it to the other ingredients. If the recipe calls for a cup of chopped onions and a cup of chopped potatoes, it's best to `chop` these vegetables before you do anything else and have all your ingredients ready at hand before you begin. If something seems confusing, *ask an adult* who knows their way around.

An *informed* Supernatural Chef

is a *smart* Supernatural Chef.

Get out all the **equipment** you need before you start to prepare each recipe. And if you learn to clean up as you go along, there won't be a big mess when you're done. Chances are you will be invited back to cook in the kitchen.

If necessary, be sure to *preheat the oven*.

And the most important thing of all—**SAFETY!** Be careful when using knives. Ask an adult to show you how to properly hold the knife when you are cutting vegetables. Of course, when you are baking or cooking on the stovetop use a potholder or kitchen mitt to avoid burns. Until you get to be an expert cook, it's better to have an adult supervising you.

COOKING TERMS (YOU NEED TO KNOW)

Bake .... Cook in an oven

Beat .... Mix vigorously with a spoon, beater or in an electric mixer

Blend .... Combine two or more ingredients thoroughly

Boil .... Cook in a liquid so hot that it bubbles and keeps on bubbling

Chop .... Cut into pieces with a knife

Cream .... Stir until creamy

DICE .... Cut into very small squares (about ¼ inch)

DOT .... Drop bits of butter here and there over food

Drain .... Pour off liquid, often using a strainer

FLOUR .... Dust greased pan with flour until well covered on the bottom and sides

Fold .... Combine gently, in an over-and-under motion, until well blended

GREASE .... Spread bottom and sides of pan with butter, oil or cooking spray

Knead .... Work dough with the hands in a punching and pressing motion

MINCE .... Chop into very tiny pieces

Sauté .... To fry quickly in a little fat

Shred .... Slice as thin as you can, lengthwise

Sift .... Put flour through a sifter to remove lumps and bumps

Simmer .... Cook over very low heat

Toss .... Mix lightly

WHIP .... Add air by beating with an eggbeater or electric mixer

Kitchen Equipment

KITCHEN EQUIPMENT

You might not need everything listed here because some items do double duty. If there is an electric mixer in your kitchen, then you can do without an **eggbeater**. Sometimes I'll use my electric blender instead of a whisk. If your oven comes with a timer, you won't need one of those either. Not everyone needs a *SALAD SPINNER* (used to get the water off the lettuce leaves you've just washed) but I can't live without mine since I eat salad every day. There are lots of fun and fancy cooking items and **gadgets** on the market, but don't get carried away, otherwise you'll have drawers filled with things you rarely use.

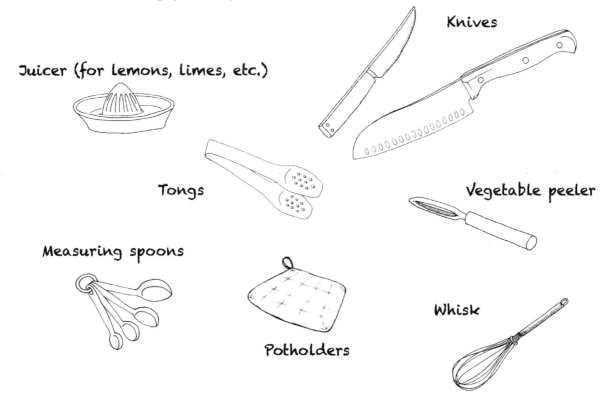

Knives

Juicer (for lemons, limes, etc.)

Tongs

Vegetable peeler

Measuring spoons

Potholders

Whisk

Other Kitchen Items:

- Apple corer
- Measuring cups
- Salad spinner
- Garlic press
- Electric mixer
- Mortar and Pestle
- Electric blender

- Strainers
- Baking pans
- Muffin tins
- Timer
- Vegetable brush
- Skillets (my favorite skillet is made from cast iron and I have used it for years)

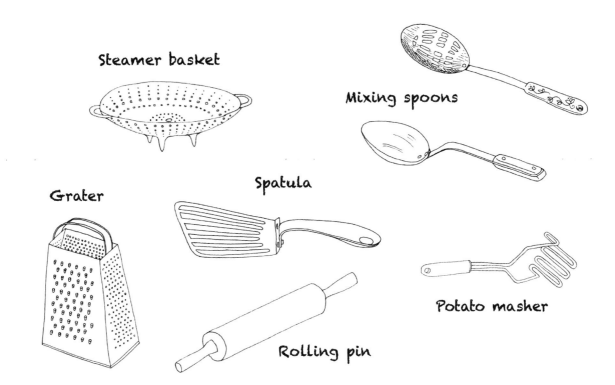

Steamer basket

Mixing spoons

Grater

Spatula

Rolling pin

Potato masher

A SUPERNATURAL WAY TO EAT

What does it mean to be a **Supernatural Kid**? It begins with a real *awareness* of the foods you purchase to prepare at home and the menu items you select at a restaurant. A Supernatural Kid eats foods that are organically grown, if possible, and prepared in a simple way. These foods have no chemical preservatives or additives like colorings and flavorings. A lot of food sold in supermarkets, especially the stuff on the shelves in the middle of the store, is processed. You can tell when something is processed because the list of ingredients on the label will be long and have a lot of words that no one can really understand. By eating organically, you and your parents might have to pay a little more and the produce might not look as perfect as what you're used to seeing, but you'll be investing in your own health and the health of our **planet**.

What are natural foods? Take a stroll through a farmers' market and you will see for yourself. Natural means that the food was **grown** without using pesticides that upset the balance of $NATURE$ and the cows were not given hormones like BST. It's important to eat foods that help us grow and stay as healthy as possible. Choosing foods from the seven Supernatural Kids' basic food groups for our meals and snacks keeps us on the road to being not just natural, but SUPERNATURAL. And the only additive we really need is LOVE. Because when you add love to your cooking, you'll become a Supernatural cook.

Here are the Supernatural Food Groups:

Fresh & Dried Fruit   Beans
Nuts & Seeds   Dairy Products
Vegetables   Eggs, Fish & Poultry
Whole Grains

FRESH & DRIED FRUIT

I never met a fruit I didn't like. If I had to name my absolute, all-time favorite I would have to say apricots. I like them so much that when I moved into my new house the first thing I did was plant an apricot tree. Even though I have to battle the squirrels that try to steal them, I still have enough left over every summer to make jars and jars of apricot jam. Friends tell me that my apricot jam is the best thing they have ever tasted.

Once, on a trip to Bali (an island in Indonesia), I tasted a strange looking fruit called a mangosteen, which doesn't look anything like a mango. That mangosteen tasted so good, I couldn't get enough of them.

Fruit supplies our bodies with important vitamins and minerals as well as fiber. They are perfect in their natural state and also fun to use in recipes. How many fruits can you name?

NUTS & SEEDS

Nuts and seeds are the perfect snack food—full of proteins, vitamins, minerals and fiber and easy to carry on hikes and trips. They can be roasted, salted and flavored all kinds of ways. I mostly like mine in their raw form, which is the healthiest way to eat them. Everyone knows about peanuts, almonds, cashews, walnuts and pecans, but have you ever tried Brazil nuts, hazelnuts, macadamias, pine nuts or pistachios? Is the coconut a nut? I wasn't certain, so I had to do some research. According to Fun Science Facts from the Library of Congress website, a coconut is a fruit, a nut AND a seed. And it has that really tasty coconut milk inside. Mother Nature is so good to us!

Seeds are just as important as nuts and they need to be eaten as fresh as possible. Seeds include pumpkin, sunflower and sesame. When you eat a wide variety of foods, you get a wide variety of nutrients. Did you know that almonds and sesame seeds are high in calcium? Everyone knows we need calcium in our diets to ensure that our bones are strong.

VEGETABLES

I'm willing to bet that at least a few times in your life, someone has said to you: "You need to eat your vegetables!" They were right. Some people think that eating French fries qualifies as eating their vegetables. NOT! I like French fries as much as anyone but I don't eat them very often. For one thing, anything fried isn't that good for me and besides, I love vegetables. And you will too, once you learn how to cook them the right way. Have you ever eaten an artichoke? They are delicious and fun to eat. You can use your fingers to pull off the leaves, dip them in melted butter, mayo, or your favorite sauce and keep going until you get to the heart, which is the best part. I won't even begin to list all the vegetables there are. There are literally thousands of varieties, from basic lettuce, carrots and celery to the more exotic taro, bamboo and sea kale. I feel lucky to live in California, where everything grows so beautifully. One of my favorite shopping trips in the world is going to the local farmers' market, where I can see all those gorgeous colors and pick out the produce I'm going to use for my dinner. When your plate is filled with all the colors of the rainbow you can be sure you are getting Supernatural nutrition. Imagine looking as beautiful as a rainbow!

WHOLE GRAINS

Grains are an important and necessary part of every diet and that is why it's so important to eat them in their whole, natural state instead of after they have been refined. When grains are refined, the best and most nutritious parts, like the bran and germ, are taken away. Whole grains include whole wheat, oats, barley, corn, quinoa, brown and wild rice, buckwheat, millet, rye and spelt. Today the use of albino (white) whole wheat is on the rise and it's getting easier to find. That's a very good thing. So many people are accustomed to eating white bread, it's now possible to use this white whole wheat, which has a milder flavor and is excellent in cakes, cookies and pancakes without sacrificing good nutrition.

Growing up in Arizona, I had the opportunity to visit the Hopi Indian Reservations many times. Corn is sacred to the Hopis and comes in many shades, even blues and pinks. The Hopi Corn Maiden is a symbol of springtime and brings peace and happiness when she appears.

Whole grains, like fruits and vegetables, contain disease-fighting phytochemicals and antioxidants as well as being a great source of fiber. People who eat whole grains on a regular basis have lower levels of cholesterol and a lower risk of obesity. And, whole grains supply our bodies with fuel so that we can be physically active. Best of all, so many delicious foods are made with whole grains, like the pancakes you will find in this book.

BEANS

If people only knew how important beans are to our health, they would probably eat more of them. They are super delicious and there are so many varieties of beans, I still have not tried them all. As a matter of fact there are over 13,000 varieties of beans around the world. Incredible! Can you imagine what a burrito would be like if beans didn't exist? And beans and rice go together like peanut butter and jelly. Beans are especially high in fiber and protein so they give our bodies a special power punch. When you combine beans with whole grains, you have a great substitute for meat. There are red beans, white beans, black beans, kidney beans, striped beans—mountains and hills of beans. They are great in soups, chili, salad and dips. Once you get to know them I'm sure you will love them just as much as I do. And some day you might even call them by their fancier name—legumes (lay-gooms).

DAIRY PRODUCTS

Dairy products include milk, butter, cheese and yogurts and can come from cows, goats and even sheep. Personally, I make an effort to buy the dairy products that are the most natural—the kind that come from animals that have not been given antibiotics and hormones. Dairy products do contain excellent nutrition in the form of fat, protein, vitamins and minerals, although some people who are lactose-intolerant cannot digest them well. Today there are many plant substitutes for milk, such as almond, soy, rice and coconut. I love almond milk and use it on my oatmeal.

EGGS, FISH & POULTRY

Some people are vegetarians, some are vegans and some eat meat. And there are others who eat mostly plant-based foods with the addition of protein from eggs, fish and poultry. Whichever choices people make in regards to what they eat, all diets need to be balanced by eating a variety of foods, to ensure that everyone gets adequate nutrition.

When my daughter Vedra was young, she had a friend named Butch. He was a fussy eater. Butch only liked pizza, hot dogs, French fries, hamburgers and spaghetti. The only vegetable he would eat was peas. One day Vedra went deep-sea fishing with her Granny and won the jackpot for catching the biggest fish—a seven-pound halibut. That halibut had been cleaned and filleted by a worker on the boat and I planned to cook it for dinner. Butch happened to be visiting. I broiled that halibut the way I usually do and urged him to try it. Guess what? Fussy eater Butch decided that he loved halibut. That broiled fish recipe is included in this book, so why not see if you can get your favorite fussy eater to expand their food experience?

MAGIC BAKED APPLES

For this recipe, I like to use Rome Beauties. I think they make perfect baked apples—big and easy to stuff. You can **experiment** with other varieties and *discover* which apples you like best. If you don't like raisins, you can substitute chopped walnuts or add some **MAGIC** of your own.

"This recipe is a family favorite in my house. I not only love the aroma of the apples when they're in the oven, but I love the comforting flavors. The hint of cinnamon really compliments the apples."

 Preheat oven to **350° F**

For each apple you will need:

1 tablespoon brown sugar
½ teaspoon butter
Dash of cinnamon
1 tablespoon raisins

Core as many apples as you want to bake. An apple corer is a great kitchen tool for removing the seeds and core. Be **careful** not to poke a hole right through the bottom of the apple, since you want to keep all the juices inside. Spoon brown sugar into each apple, and then DOT with butter and raisins. Sprinkle apples with cinnamon.

Next, place apples in a baking pan and pour about ½ inch of water or apple juice in the pan. Carefully place pan in the oven and **bake** for **45 minutes.** Serve apples hot or cold, plain or with yogurt or *whipped cream.* They're great for breakfast, dessert or a snack.

Swedish Pancakes

SWEDISH PANCAKES

These pancakes, which are really more like **crepes**, were my favorite when I was a kid and then became my daughter's favorite. She's all grown-up now but she still begs me to make them for her. I think they are great because they can be served with so many different **toppings** or filled with your **favorite** fruits. The extra bonus is that they are high in protein.

"These pancakes are so simple, and can be topped with anything. I love to top these pancakes with homemade fruit jams, and coconut nectar."

1 cup milk
4 eggs
1 cup whole wheat pastry flour
½ teaspoon salt
6 teaspoons butter **for cooking**

Place the milk, eggs, flour and salt into the blender and blend until smooth. Using the blender makes this so easy.

Melt 1 teaspoon of the butter in a non-stick skillet. When hot, pour ½ cup batter into the skillet and swirl around until the entire bottom of the skillet is coated. Using a spatula, peek under the pancake and when it starts to turn golden, flip the pancake over and cook until the other side is golden. Continue like this until you have made about **6 pancakes**. It's easy peasy.

TOPPING SUGGESTIONS:

Brown sugar with lemon juice
Maple syrup
Your favorite fruit jam
Honey

Cheese Omelet

CHEESE OMELET

What a perfect food to prepare for breakfast, lunch or even dinner. This is one of those basic recipes that everyone really needs to know. It's nice to **surprise** someone on a special day when you want to serve them breakfast in bed—just add some whole wheat toast and fresh fruit and watch them smile.

"This is one of my favorite breakfast recipes. I love to eat eggs poached, sunny side up, and even scrambled. But my favorite way to have eggs is in an omelet. This recipe isn't too cheesy, and that's what I love about it. To pump up the nutrients you can add any of your favorite veggies. I like to add spinach."

3 eggs
1 tablespoon milk
⅛ teaspoon salt
1 tablespoon butter
⅓ cup grated cheese like Parmesan, Monterey Jack **or** Cheddar

In a bowl, whisk the eggs, milk and salt together.

Next, **melt** the butter in a nonstick medium-sized skillet, swirling it around so the butter coats the bottom and all sides of the pan. Pour the egg mixture into the pan and *swirl* it some more so it goes up on the sides a bit.

As the eggs start to cook, use a rubber spatula to lift the sides of the omelet so some of the runny part gets underneath to cook. (Always remember to use rubber spatulas on nonstick pans so they won't get scratched.)

When you don't see any more runny parts, *sprinkle* the cheese on one half of the omelet then use your spatula to fold it over so it looks like a taco. It's done! Wasn't that **easy**?

EGGTASTIC FRITATTA

"Frittatas are eggs dressed in their Sunday best. Once you get used to the idea of making eggs in the oven and once you see how beautiful they look on a plate you may never scramble eggs on the stovetop again."

 Preheat oven to **375° F**

2 tablespoons olive oil	**1 cup** tomatoes, **chopped**
1 cup cubed turkey ham	**1 teaspoon** dried thyme
2 cloves garlic, **crushed**	**salt &** pepper **to taste**
½ medium onion, chopped	**4 oz** Gouda cheese, **cubed**
1 cup shredded brussel sprouts	**4** eggs, **beaten**

Haile's Recipe

Heat olive oil in a skillet and fry the turkey ham until browned, about **2 minutes**. Stir in the garlic and onion and **sauté** for another **2 minutes**. Next add the shredded Brussels sprouts and continue sautéing for another **2-3 minutes.**

Then *stir* in the chopped tomatoes. Season with salt, pepper and thyme.   mixture to a buttered baking dish or pie plate. Next mix in the cubed Gouda cheese, and then pour in the beaten eggs.

If you like, egg whites can also be used. *Bake* for 20 minutes or until firm.

MONKEY MUFFINS

These banana muffins are the hit of the **JUNGLE**. You will have to use a few bowls in the process of making them, but they are so worth the little bit of extra effort.

"I love to eat these muffins for a fruity treat. I especially like the different textures, like crunchy walnut, creamy banana, and chewy raisins. YUM!"

 Preheat oven to **350° F**

1 cup butter **(2 sticks), at room temperature**	**½ teaspoon** salt
1 cup raw sugar **(also called turbinado)**	**½ teaspoon** cinnamon
2 eggs	**¼ teaspoon** nutmeg
1 teaspoon vanilla extract	**3 very ripe** bananas, **mashed (use a fork)**
1 cup unbleached all purpose flour	**½ cup** buttermilk
¾ cup whole wheat flour	**½ cup chopped** walnuts
1 teaspoon baking powder	**½ cup** raisins

In a large mixing bowl or the bowl of an electric mixer, *cream* together the butter and sugar. Add the eggs and **beat** until well blended. Then stir in the vanilla.

In a separate bowl, **sift** together the flours, baking powder and salt. Add the flour mixture to the butter mixture, a little bit at a time. Next mix in the mashed bananas and buttermilk. Finally stir in the walnuts and raisins. Spoon this mixture into cupcake papers in a muffin tin and **bake** in the oven for **20-25 minutes**, until golden brown on top. Allow them to cool a bit before taking that first bite.

❧ **Makes about 16 muffins**

ZANY ZUCCHINI BREAD

This bread is more like *cake*. It's easy to make and really delicious. Around my house it doesn't even last a day. And it's a great way to use zucchini from your **garden**. Did you know the largest zucchini ever recorded weighed in at sixty-five pounds? Talk about a *zany* zucchini!

"I love zucchini, whether it's in a veggie dish or for dessert. I love the idea of incorporating veggies into desserts. I can't get enough of this zucchini bread."

Preheat oven to **325° F**

2 eggs
½ **cup** vegetable oil
1 cup raw sugar
1 cup grated zucchini
1 teaspoon vanilla extract
1 ½ cups whole wheat flour
½ **teaspoon** salt
¼ **teaspoon** baking powder
½ **teaspoon** baking soda
1 teaspoon cinnamon
½ **cup** chopped walnuts or pecans

Beat eggs in a large mixing bowl. Add oil, sugar, zucchini and vanilla and beat again. Then add all the dry ingredients (flour, salt, baking powder, baking soda, cinnamon and nuts) and mix well with a spoon.

Pour mixture into a *greased* loaf pan (cooking spray works well here) and **bake for 50-60 minutes**, or until a knife inserted into the bread comes out clean. Let bread COOL before cutting it or removing it from pan.

CRUNCHY HONEY GRANOLA

Crunchy Honey Granola

"It is so much fun to make homemade granola. I love the process of making granola with my family; we get our hands dirty and just have fun together. But my favorite part about making this dish is eating it."

 Preheat oven to **250° F**

> **2 ½ cups** rolled oats
> **½ cup dried** milk powder
> **½ cup** wheat germ
> **½ cup** shredded coconut **(unsweetened)**
> **½ teaspoon** salt
> **½ cup** vegetable oil
> **½ cup** honey
> **1 teaspoon** vanilla

MIX the first five ingredients together in a large bowl and then set aside.

In another bowl, mix the oil, honey and vanilla and pour this mixture into the dry ingredients. Blend until dry ingredients are well coated.

SPREAD your granola mixture on a large baking tray, place in the oven and bake for one hour. Every **15 minutes**, carefully turn the granola over with a spatula, so that all the grains will bake. When granola is golden brown, remove from oven and allow to cool. When cool, store in a jar or plastic bag. **Eat** granola with raisins and milk or by itself as a snack.

FRUITY QUINOA BREAKFAST PARFAIT

Parfaits are *fancy*, tasty, healthy and so super simple to make. You can make this **for friends**, for brunch or even if you want to surprise your parents with an easy yet thoughtful breakfast in bed. If you have mint on hand, or a strawberry, you can top for a little bit of added **color.**

Haile's Recipe

For each parfait you will need:

1 cup cooked quinoa, chilled
½ cup vanilla Greek yogurt
¼ cup blueberries
1 teaspoon chia seeds
1 teaspoon flax seeds

✄ Parfait glasses come in many shapes and sizes... you can choose your own!

LAYER the ingredients in a parfait glass and serve for a healthy breakfast.

*Be creative! add things you love, like:

Bananas
Apples
Peaches
Coconut
Cashews

Fruit purée

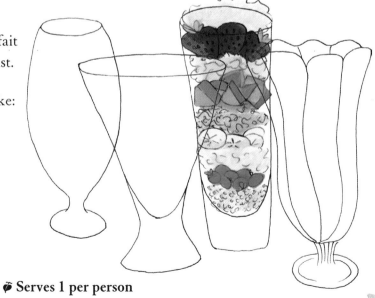

🍎 Serves 1 per person

WHOLE WHEAT CHEDDAR BISCUITS

"Yummy! Way better tasting than any packaged biscuits you could buy. It's so fun to make too."

 Preheat oven to **400° F**

2 cups whole wheat flour
2 tablespoons baking powder
½ teaspoon baking soda
1 tablespoon raw sugar
½ teaspoon salt
4 tablespoons cold butter
¾ cup buttermilk
¾ cup finely grated sharp Cheddar cheese

In a large mixing bowl, combine the flour, baking powder, baking soda, sugar and salt. Using a pastry blender CUT in the butter and until the mixture looks crumbly. Next add in the buttermilk and the cheese and stir just until the dry ingredients are wet. It's important not to over mix. Use an ice cream scoop to drop golf ball-sized balls of dough onto an ungreased baking sheet. **Bake** for **12-15 minutes** or until the tops of the biscuits turn light brown.

❧ **Makes 12 biscuits**

SALSA SURPRISE

This salsa, made without tomatoes, may not be what you are accustomed to but it is *yummy* and you will love SURPRISING your friends and family with your fruity creation.

"I love this recipe because it is a unique twist on traditional salsa. I really enjoy the taste of the mangoes; it is just so sweet and fresh. I enjoy this salsa on tortilla chips all the time."

1 mango, **peeled and diced**
½ fresh pineapple, **peeled and diced**
⅓ **cup red onion, chopped fine**
2 tablespoons fresh cilantro, **chopped**
2 tablespoons fresh lime juice

Place all ingredients into a bowl, gently **toss** and serve with cinnamon chips.

🌿 You can also use peaches, nectarines and papayas.

SMOOTHIES

Smoothies are so e a s y to make you almost don't need a recipe. But without a basic guideline you might have too much or too little, make it too runny or too thick. So I'm going to start you off by giving you some of my personal favorites. Try them...then **invent** your own. These delicious drinks pack a lot of nutrition and they can be made as a snack or even as a whole meal in a glass. Sometimes I take mine to go when I'm in a hurry.

To make any of the smoothie recipes that follow, simply place the ingredients into the jar of a blender, put on the lid and blend at medium-high speed until smooth. Remember, **NEVER** stick anything into the blender (like a spoon) when it's on. Turn it off and then you can mix it around if it's a little thick. I like to use frozen unsweetened fruit since it makes the smoothies colder and more like a *milk shake*. All smoothie recipes serve two.

For frozen bananas, **peel** first and wrap tightly in plastic wrap before freezing.

Nutty Yogurt Smoothie

"Nutty, sweet and super quick. This is the perfect grab and go breakfast."

1 cup apple juice
1 cup vanilla yogurt
1 banana (fresh or frozen)
1 tablespoon smooth peanut butter
Sprinkling of cinnamon

Almond Ambrosia

"I love almond milk and it just goes so well with the fruits in this smoothie. This is a great ingredient combination. Delicious!"

2 cups almond milk
1 frozen banana
4 frozen strawberries
A few chunks of frozen pineapple

Berries and Cream

"I think berries are great, and when added to ice-cream it is like heaven in a cup."

Tropical Smoothie

1 ½ cups pineapple juice
1 frozen banana
A chunk of frozen papaya
½ cup coconut juice

1 cup milk
1 cup natural vanilla ice cream
1 cup frozen mixed berries (strawberries, raspberries and blueberries)

SANDWICHES

Here is a selection of **tasty** sandwiches for you to try. By now you know that when a recipe calls for bread, that means the real whole-wheat or **whole grain** kind, not the airy cotton-puff variety. Read the bread `label` and make sure there are no chemicals and preservatives added.

Two slices of whole grain bread
Peanut butter **(smooth or crunchy)**
Honey (about one teaspoon)
Banana slices (½ banana**)**

NUTTY HONEYANA

"Mmmmm! I just can't get enough of PB and B sandwiches, and with that special touch of honey, it is just the best."

HAPPY HIPPIE

"Such a yummy sandwich. I love avocados and I consider myself a cheese-head, so this is my dream sandwich. Cool name too."

Two slices of whole grain **or whole wheat bread**
Avocado **slices**
Cheese slices
Alfalfa sprouts or lettuce
Mayonnaise

Two slices of your favorite bread
A few thin slices of nitrate-free sliced turkey
Slice of Swiss cheese
Some mayo **or mustard**
Lettuce or alfalfa sprouts
Tomato slice

DELI-CIOUS TURKEY

"I love sandwiches, especially when they are totally customizable. You can put anything imaginable on this sandwich."

SWEET POTATO CHIPS

Did you know that sweet potatoes are one of the most **nutritious** vegetables around? They are one of my *favorites* and I love preparing them this way. In fact, it's hard to stop eating these sweet potato chips.

"Not only are these chips much tastier than any other chips sold at the store, but they are also much healthier. I am able to control the amount of salt and oil that I use for my homemade chips. I could munch on them all day."

 Preheat oven to **400° F**

4 medium size sweet potatoes
2 tablespoons olive oil
½ teaspoon salt

Cut off the ends of each sweet potato and then peel them. Slice carefully into rounds about ¼ inch thick. Place the slices into a bowl and *pour* the olive oil over them. Then add the salt. Mix them up with your hands (you remembered to wash your hands before you got started, right?) so all the slices are coated with the oil.

Spread the slices out on a baking sheet and bake for **15-20 minutes** until *CRISPY*. Use a spatula to remove them from the baking sheet and let them cool a bit before eating.

oops...

SESAME BREADSTICKS

Did you know that sesame seeds pop from their hull as soon as they are **ripe**, magically scattering in all directions? Maybe that is why "Open Sesame" is the secret password to open the doors to hidden treasures. You will have fun making Sesame Breadsticks. You could even try to make them in the shape of a key.

"I love being able to make my own breadsticks, they are a tiny bit sweet and perfectly crunchy."

1 packet (1 tablespoon) dry yeast
1 teaspoon raw sugar
3 cups whole wheat flour
1 tablespoon sea salt
1 cup water
2 tablespoons olive oil

1 egg, beaten
1 tablespoon sesame seeds

First, *dissolve* yeast in ¼ cup warm water, then stir in 1 teaspoon raw sugar. Let stand for **10 minutes**. The mixture should **double** in size.

In a large mixing bowl, blend the flour and salt. Add the yeast mixture, 1 cup of water and the olive oil. First mix well with a spoon, then use your clean hands to form the dough. Set the timer and knead the dough for **5 minutes**. Kneading means bashing and smashing the dough around. Form the dough into a ball, place in the bowl, cover with a cloth and let it rise for **1 hour** in a warm place (about **90° F**).

 Preheat oven to **400° F**

While the oven is heating, take your ball of dough and start *pinching* off pieces until you form **12 balls,** each one about the size of a golf ball.

Using both your hands, **ROLL** each ball into a tube shape about 10 inches long. Place these on an oiled baking sheet. Using a pastry brush, carefully brush the top of the breadsticks with the beaten egg. Next sprinkle each one with sesame seeds.

Place them in the oven and bake for **12-15 minutes**, or until the breadsticks are a nice *golden* brown.

CREAMY VEGGIE DIP

This dip doubles as a SAUCE for steamed veggies too. It's so good you will end up eating **lots** of carrot and celery sticks, just so you can keep dipping. Once the cream cheese is softened, it only takes about two minutes to make.

"So simple and yummy."

4 ounces of softened **cream cheese (low-fat works great)**
Juice of one lemon
2 tablespoons of Tamari soy sauce **(low-sodium variety is perfect)**

Leave the cream cheese out of the refrigerator to softEN it. When soft, put in a mixing bowl and *cream* until smooth. Stir in the lemon juice and the tamari and blend until creamy. Start *dipping*.

BLUE CORN BREAD

Using a heated dish to bake this cornbread is the secret to a nice **crusty** bottom.

"I love corn bread. Using blue corn is super unique, but most definitely as delicious."

Preheat oven to **400° F**

1 cup blue corn meal	**1 cup milk or** buttermilk
1 cup whole wheat flour	**2 eggs**
1 tablespoon baking powder	**½ cup** vegetable oil
1 teaspoon salt	**¼ cup honey**
¼ teaspoon nutmeg	**1 tablespoon soft butter**

Mix the first five (dry) ingredients in a large bowl. Using a blender or mixer, mix all liquids (milk, eggs, oil and honey) and add liquid mixture to the dry mixture. STIR until all ingredients are moistened. Don't over mix the batter.

Use 1 tablespoon of butter to GREASE an 8-inch baking dish. Place empty dish in preheated oven. When the pan is hot (about **10 minutes**), *carefully* remove it from the oven and quickly pour in the batter, then return dish to oven.

Bake for **20-25 minutes**, until cornbread is nicely BROWNED and a toothpick inserted in the center comes out clean.

🍎 Serves 6

Hoping for a good harvest.

PEANUT HONEY BALLS

This treat is great for snacking, high in protein, fun to make and mighty *tasty*.

"Great snack! Sweet, plus pretty good for you. I love rolling these up and taking them to school for my snack."

> 1 cup thick honey
> 1 cup peanut butter (smooth or crunchy)
> 2 cups powdered milk
> 1 cup peanuts, finely chopped (they can be roasted and salted or unsalted)

Pour the honey into a mixing bowl and gradually blend in the peanut butter. Mix in the dry milk powder. (It's probably best to mix with a fork.)

Form the mixture into small balls with your clean hands. Then ROLL each ball in the chopped peanuts and place on waxed paper on a cookie sheet. Chill in the refrigerator until they are firm and ready to munch on.

FROZEN POPS ON A STICK

In England they're called "ice lollies." I love that name. It's important to drink lots of liquids and since popsicles are really frozen liquids, they're a fun way to hydrate. All kinds of fruit juices make great pops and mixing different kinds together creates new tastes and colors. You can freeze pops in paper cups or in popsicle molds.

"I love popsicles. I also really enjoy being able to mix up any fruit and make a pop out of it."

Try these **combinations** and look for juices that don't have added sugar or high fructose corn syrup. Remember, it's important to always read labels.

Apple **and grape**	Papaya **and** pineapple
Orange **and grape**	**Guava and** passion fruit
Pineapple **and orange**	

You can also make great pops out of yogurt. It makes *creamy* pops—a little more filling too. You can use flavored yogurt or mix plain yogurt with fruit juice.

Here are two of my favorite combinations:

1 cup plain yogurt
½ cup grape juice

1 cup plain yogurt
½ cup pineapple juice
¼ cup papaya juice

For fun, try adding small pieces of banana, grapes or strawberries to your yogurt pops. Simply mix juices and/or yogurt well and pour into cups. Since liquids expand as they freeze, never fill cups or molds all the way. Leave some room at the top. If you are using paper cups, put a small piece of plastic wrap TIGHTLY over the top of the cup, make a slit in the middle and place the popsicle stick into it. That keeps the stick in the middle when they are done. Freeze for about **2-3 hours**. *Waiting* is the only hard part about making popsicles.

BAKED PARMESAN ZUCCHINI STICKS

"These are a great sub for fries. They are crispy, and not too salty. They are just right."

Preheat oven to **450° F**

Cooking spray	¼ **cup grated Parmesan cheese**
4 medium zucchini	½ **teaspoon dried** oregano
¼ **cup** whole wheat flour	¼ **teaspoon** garlic powder
2 eggs, beaten	½ **teaspoon** salt
1 cup breadcrumbs	¼ **teaspoon** black pepper

Begin by covering a baking sheet with cooking spray and set it aside. Then WASH and dry the zucchini and trim off the ends. Slice each zucchini down the middle then slice each half into thirds so they look like long, skinny sticks.

Arrange three bowls in a **row**. The first bowl is for the whole wheat flour. Bowl number two is for the beaten eggs and in bowl number three mix the breadcrumbs, Parmesan, oregano, garlic powder, salt and pepper. Now you have your zucchini assembly line.

Dip the zucchini sticks in the flour, then the egg and finally the breadcrumb mixture. Try to coat them well. Lay them on the cookie sheet. When all the zucchini have been breaded, *bake* them for **10 minutes.** Carefully turn them over with a spatula and bake them for another **10 minutes.** (Remember, the oven will be **hot!**) Serve them hot from the oven.

BAKED ACORN SQUASH

I especially like going to the farmers' markets in the fall, when all the winter squashes are on display. There are so many **varieties**, in all the fall colors of greens, yellows and oranges; it excites me to think of all the various dishes I can make with them. This is one of the easiest and *tastiest* to make and it looks adorable on a dinner plate.

"I love this recipe, especially when the squash are in season. This recipe captures both sweet and savory flavors. This is a great seasonal recipe."

 Preheat oven to **375° F**

1 acorn squash **(serves 2 people)**
2 tablespoons butter
2 tablespoons maple syrup
½ teaspoon cinnamon
½ teaspoon salt

Wash the squash then, most definitely, ask an adult to help you cut it in half. It requires a large, sharp knife. After that, you can **scoop** out the seeds with a spoon.

DOT with 1 tablespoon of butter and 1 tablespoon of maple syrup inside each squash half. Sprinkle with a little salt and cinnamon and place the squash on a roasting pan or baking dish. *Pour* about a half-inch of water into the pan or dish and place in the oven.

Bake for **45 minutes** or until the squash is tender and you can put a fork through it.

 That's it! Yum!

CURRIED SWEET CARROTS

"Curry is one of my favorite spices, and when paired with sweet veggies like carrots, it is perfect. This is a great side dish that satisfies your sweet tooth and has the added benefit of zesty flavor from the curry."

8 medium size carrots
2 tablespoons butter
1 tablespoon mild curry powder
½ teaspoon salt
2 tablespoons light brown sugar

Peel, then *slice* the carrots into rounds. **Steam** them using a steamer basket over medium heat about **10 minutes**, or until tender. **Drain** them into a colander.

Melt the butter in a saucepan, then stir in the curry powder and salt. Add the light brown sugar and stir until a sauce is formed. **Toss** in the carrots and enjoy.

Serves 4-6

CHEESY PAPAS

This is an old-fashioned potato side dish that never goes out of style. It goes perfectly with a nice salad for a light dinner.

"Potatoes are a favorite of mine, and when paired with cheese, I am so happy. The paprika in this dish really compliments the Gruyere and Parmesan."

Preheat oven to **350° F**

> 2 **large Russet potatoes, peeled and cut into ¼ inch slices**
> ½ **cup of grated Gruyere or your favorite cheese**
> ½ **cup fresh grated** Parmesan cheese
> ¾ **cup milk** (regular or low-fat)
> 1 **teaspoon** salt
> ½ **teaspoon** black pepper
> ¼ **teaspoon paprika**
> 2 ½ **tablespoons** butter

BUTTER a 1 quart baking dish with 1 teaspoon of the butter, then **layer** the bottom with potatoes, sprinkle with both the cheeses, then another layer of potatoes sprinkled with the cheese and finally another layer of potatoes and cheese.

Pour milk over the potatoes and sprinkle over the salt, pepper and paprika. Finally DOT the top with the butter.

Bake for **1 hour** or until brown and **crispy** on top and potatoes are fork-tender.

⌐ Serves 4-6

SAUTEED BRUSSEL SPROUTS

There is something so charming about brussel sprouts. They resemble tiny cabbages and grow on a long stalk. Whenever they sell those stalks of brussel sprouts at the farmers' market, I can't resist. And they are super healthy. While they might seem like more of an adult food, they'll become a favorite of yours when made the Supernatural way.

1 pound brussel sprouts
2 tablespoons olive oil
1 tablespoon butter
1 tablespoon Tamari soy sauce
½ teaspoon salt
¼ teaspoon black pepper

Begin by cutting off the brown ends of the brussel sprouts and peeling off any yellow leaves. Then, using a small knife, carefully slice them so they are all shredded.

Melt the butter and olive oil in a heavy skillet and add the shredded brussel sprouts. Keep stirring them until they start to look wilted. This is the only time I am going to tell you that it's okay if they scorch a little because the slightly burned bits of the brussel sprouts are so good.

Stir in the Tamari soy sauce, salt and pepper and you have a wonderful SIDE DISH, especially for a holiday meal.

❧ Serves 4

When it rains, we pour. Soup, that is.

Sedona Tortilla Soup

SEDONA TORTILLA SOUP

I was born and raised in the Southwest so I love a good tortilla soup. Every time I make this people come back for more. This is something your entire family will love. Around my house we keep the Tabasco sauce handy for people who like their tortilla soup really SPICY.

"This soup says Arizona to me, I love it! My favorite addition is the tortilla strips."

1 pound boneless, skinless chicken breast tenders
1 tablespoon cumin
1 tablespoon chile powder
2 tablespoons olive oil
1 large red onion, chopped
½ red bell pepper, chopped
2 or 3 cloves garlic, minced
1 teaspoon oregano
1 cup tomato sauce
6 cups of chicken broth
1 ½ teaspoons salt
½ teaspoon black pepper
Juice of 2 or 3 limes
½ cup chopped fresh cilantro
6 corn tortillas, sliced into strips
1 cup crumbled Cotija cheese,
Queso Fresco or your favorite grated Cheddar

Start by *cutting* the chicken in strips. I like to use my kitchen scissors for this. (When working with raw chicken it's important to **wash** your hands with warm water and soap after handling it as well as washing the cutting board.) Put the spices, the cumin and chile powder, into a bowl, mix and then toss the chicken in the spice mixture and rub them around until the pieces are all well coated.

Next heat the olive oil in a stockpot and **sauté** the chicken in it for about **5 minutes**. Then stir in the onion, bell pepper and garlic and continue sautéing for about **10 minutes more**, until the onions and pepper are soft. Add the oregano, tomato sauce, chicken broth, salt and pepper and let the mixture come to a full boil. Then lower the heat to simmer, cover with a lid and cook for **30 minutes**.

Finally, stir in the lime juice, the chopped cilantro and the corn tortillas. Cook for a **few minutes more**, until the tortillas *FALL* apart and thicken the soup. Serve with the crumbled or grated cheese on top. **OLE!**

🌿 **Serves 6**

Has anyone ever told you that you look like a fork?

FROG POND FARM SOUP

One September, I was visiting friends who lived on a farm in Upstate New York. We took an amazing drive through the countryside and came upon a rustic roadside vegetable stand called Frog Pond Farm and with a great name like that I just had to stop. There were bushels of freshly picked vegetables for sale and I bought some. I dashed back to my friends' home to create this **special** soup, which has been a **favorite** in my family ever since.

"The soup has a cool name and tastes just as good. The sage and nutmeg create an amazing flavor base for the soup, and the sweetness from the corn and squash are a great compliment."

2 tablespoons butter
1 large onion, **chopped**
3 ears of corn, with kernels cut from the cobs
6 cups vegetable **or** chicken stock
2 medium size potatoes, peeled and diced
1 butternut squash, peeled, seeded and chopped into chunks
1 teaspoon rubbed sage
½ teaspoon ground nutmeg
1 teaspoon salt

Melt the butter in a large stockpot and stir in the onion. Sauté the onion until golden. Add the corn kernels and sauté a **few minutes** more. Next, add the potatoes and the butternut squash and then pour in the stock. Stir in the sage, nutmeg and salt. Lower the heat, cover with a lid and **simmer** the soup for 1 hour.

Remove the lid and using a potato masher, MASH the potatoes and squash well. This will make the soup a little CHUNKY instead of being pureed. I love chunks in my soup...mmmmmmmm.

Serves 4-6

SPLIT PEA SOUP

This soup is one that the whole family will enjoy and will WARM everyone up on cold days and nights. A countryside favorite, pea soup was first enjoyed over two thousand years ago on the streets of Athens. Soup might seem like a simple dish, but this recipe takes *sixteen* different ingredients to create the perfect pea soup. It's not complicated, and when you see how all these flavors come together, it's a little Supernatural MAGIC on your stovetop.

"I love this soup because it is loaded with so many fresh veggies. Its very comforting and packs a delicious and nutritious punch."

2 cups split peas	½ teaspoon dried rosemary
8 cups water, vegetable broth or chicken broth	1 teaspoon marjoram
1 large bay leaf	½ teaspoon rubbed sage
1 large onion, chopped	¼ teaspoon dry mustard
1 carrot, diced	½ teaspoon paprika
2 stalks celery, chopped	2 tablespoons butter
2 cloves garlic, pressed	1 teaspoon salt
1 teaspoon thyme	½ teaspoon black pepper

Combine the first seven ingredients in a large heavy pot and bring to a boil. Then lower the heat, cover the pot and simmer for **45 minutes**. Stir soup occasionally and check to make sure the water isn't boiling out.

Finally, add all the herbs, spices, butter and salt and simmer for **15 minutes** more. Let soup sit, covered for **10 minutes** before serving.

❧ Serves 6

SWEET AND SASSY SLAW

This is an especially DELICIOUS cole slaw and it makes a great side dish.

2 cups shredded red cabbage
2 cups shredded Napa or Savoy cabbage
½ bunch cilantro, washed and chopped (about ¼ cup)
6 sweet Gherkin pickles, chopped fine
Juice of 1 lemon
¼ cup sour cream
¼ cup mayonnaise

Mix all ingredients together in a salad bowl and serve.

❧ Serves 6

"I love this salad dressing, not only because it's so simple, but also because of its tangy and salty flavors. Tamari is gluten-free, so everyone can enjoy."

NANCY'S FAVORITE SALAD DRESSING:

Place all ingredients in a small jar. Pop on the lid, close it **tightly** and shake it well. Drizzle on your favorite salad.

8 tablespoons olive oil
2 tablespoons rice vinegar
2 teaspoons Tamari soy sauce

MEXIQUINOA SALAD

Okay, so I made up that word. Quinoa (pronounced "keen-wah") is an ANCIENT grain that comes from the Andes in South America. The Incas ate it, along with corn and beans. It is gluten-free and has more protein than any other grain. It's truly Supernatural and super delicious. There are so many ways to cook it. Maybe you'll invent one of your own recipes after trying this one.

"This salad reminds of my own Quinoa Salad. But what makes this salad different from my own is the cumin, and I love this addition. This is a family favorite in my home."

1 cup quinoa
2 cups vegetable or chicken broth
½ teaspoon sea salt
1 cup cooked corn kernels
1 cup cooked black beans
3 green onions, sliced
Small bunch cilantro leaves, chopped
2 tablespoons olive oil
Zest* and juice of 1 lime
½ teaspoon ground cumin

Place 1 cup of quinoa and 2 cups broth (or water) in a saucepan, add sea salt and bring to a full boil. Reduce the heat to simmer, cover and cook until all the broth or water is absorbed, about **15- 20 minutes**. When done, the grains will look almost clear. Fluff with a fork and let stand until cool.

Place the quinoa into a salad bowl, add the corn, black beans, sliced onions, cilantro, olive oil, lime zest and juice, cumin and salt and pepper to taste.

* **Zest** means the finely grated skin of the lime. It is best to grate the lime before juicing it.

SOBA NOODLE SALAD WITH PEANUT DRESSING

"I love soba noodles. The addition of carrots and ginger really makes this dish awesome. Then topped off with some Peanut sauce. Talk about YUMMY!"

8 ounces buckwheat soba noodles
3 green onions, sliced thin
1 medium size carrot, peeled and grated or shredded
¼ cup chopped cilantro

Peanut Dressing:

⅓ cup oil (olive **or** peanut)
¼ cup rice vinegar
2 tablespoons Tamari soy sauce
½ teaspoon garlic powder
Juice of 1 lime
4 tablespoons natural peanut butter (smooth or chunky)
1 tablespoon honey
1 teaspoon fresh grated ginger root

Add the buckwheat noodles to a pot of boiling water and **simmer** for about **8 minutes**, or until tender. Use your timer so you do not overcook them. Drain noodles and rinse them with cold water. Put noodles into a salad bowl and toss in the onions, carrots and cilantro.

Place all dressing ingredients into an electric blender and blend until smooth. **Pour** over noodles and vegetables and it's ready to be eaten.

Serves 4-6

QUINOA TABBOULI

Quinoa is part of the "goosefoot" family. It has nothing to do with geese or feet. And it's not really a cereal or grain. It's actually a *seed*. And it's related to spinach and beetroot and originated in South America. Some call it a "superfood" because of its fairly high **PROTEIN** content. The United Nations General Assembly called 2013 "The Year of the Quinoa" because of its prominent use as a food source all over the world. This tabouli packs *FLAVOR* and protein in one dish and it's pretty easy to make.

Haile's Recipe

2 cups quinoa, rinsed well
½ cup fresh lemon juice
1 garlic clove, minced
½ cup olive oil
1 tablespoon seasoning blend
1 teaspoon salt

3 English or Persian cucumbers, cut into ¼" slices
1 pink cherry tomatoes, halved
1 medium red onion, chopped finely
½ bunch flat-leaf parsley, chopped finely
½ bunch fresh mint leaves, chopped finely

Cook Quinoa according to package instructions. Remove from heat and let stand, covered, for 5 minutes. Fluff with a fork. Let cool, then transfer the quinoa to a salad bowl.

Next **whisk** lemon juice and garlic in a small bowl. Gradually whisk in olive oil. Season the dressing with seasoning blend and salt.

Add cucumbers, tomatoes, red onion, parsley and mint to bowl with quinoa and **toss**. Finally mix in dressing to coat.

🌿 Serves 6-8

Cucumber & Yogurt Salad

CUCUMBER AND YOGURT SALAD

Growing up Armenian, my *family* had this salad with dinner often, since my father made his own yogurt. As I traveled around the world, I discovered that many other cultures made the same yogurt salad, with a few variations. I like it best with *homegrown* cucumbers, especially the crunchy Japanese and Persian varieties.

"This salad is just so fresh and vibrant. The cucumbers help keep me hydrated too. It's a win win meal."

3 cups plain low-fat yogurt
1 cup of chopped, peeled cucumbers **(½ inch cubes)**
1 teaspoon dried mint leaves, **crushed**

Place all the ingredients into a salad bowl and blend together. That's it.

❧ Serves 4

Dinner is served!

Turkey meatballs are fun to make and so tasty to eat. Without the BBQ sauce you could even put them into the spaghetti sauce I hope you learned to make in the first **Supernatural Kids Cookbook**. Or you could just eat them with brown rice and a salad.

"These meatballs are super tasty, and flavored with just the right amount of herbs. Delish!"

 Preheat oven to **375° F**

1 lb. ground turkey	**¼ teaspoon** black pepper
1 small onion, **chopped fine**	**¼ teaspoon** garlic powder
½ medium zucchini, **grated (about ½ cup)**	**½ teaspoon** thyme
1 egg, beaten	**½ teaspoon** rubbed sage
½ cup whole wheat bread crumbs	**½ cup of your favorite natural** BBQ sauce
1 teaspoon salt	

In a mixing bowl, blend all the ingredients except the BBQ sauce together and mix well. You can use your hands or a spoon. Then form balls by **ROLLING** the mixture between your palms and place the meatballs in an 8-inch square-baking dish. Pour the BBQ sauce on top of them and bake in the oven for **45 minutes.**

VEGETABLE PUDDING

Vegetable pudding is an excellent way to use leftover *vegetables*. You can experiment and use a combination or a DIFFERENT vegetable every time.

"This dish is so flavorful and delicious. It's cheesy, packed with plenty veggies, and really easy to make too. You can substitute any of your favorite veggies."

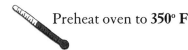 Preheat oven to **350° F**

4 cups of vegetables—corn, **(cut fresh from the cob)** broccoli, green beans, **carrots, etc. (steamed and chopped)**
4 green onions **(scallions) chopped (white and green parts)**
4 eggs, lightly beaten
½ cup milk
3 tablespoons melted butter
1 cup grated Jack cheese **(about ¾ lb.)**
⅓ cup breadcrumbs
1 teaspoon salt
½ teaspoon pepper

In a large bowl, combine vegetable, green onions, eggs, milk, butter, ½ cup of the cheese, breadcrumbs, salt and pepper. Mix gently but thoroughly. **Grease** or spray a heavy medium-sized casserole dish. *Pour* mixture into it and sprinkle remaining cheese on top.

Bake uncovered for **40 minutes** or until center is "set." Cool for **10 minutes** before serving.

⌐ Serves 6

BAKED CHICKEN TENDERS

Baked Chicken Tenders

Most kids love chicken tenders and *chicken nuggets*. Everyone knows that. What everyone might not know is that most of them are made from ingredients that don't have much to do with real chickens and they are prepared in a way that has a bad effect on health. Not these chicken nuggets. Once you make them, they'll likely become a healthy family favorite.

"This is the best replacement for chicken nuggets. Crunchy and spiced up. I especially love the touch of Tamari soy sauce."

 Preheat the oven to **400° F**

> 1 ½ lbs. boneless, skinless chicken breast **tenders**
> **1 cup** buttermilk
> **½ teaspoon** garlic powder
> **½ teaspoon** paprika
> **1 tablespoon** Tamari soy sauce
> **2 cups whole wheat bread crumbs**
> **1 teaspoon of your favorite seasoning salt, like Spike**

Place the chicken pieces into a bowl or baking dish. **Stir** the garlic powder, paprika and soy sauce into the buttermilk and pour it over the chicken pieces. Cover and place in the refrigerator for at least **an hour,** to *marinate*.

Stir seasoning salt into the breadcrumbs and put them on a platter. Take chicken pieces and DIP them into the breadcrumbs until they are completely coated. Put these pieces on a non-stick baking sheet and put in the oven. Set the timer for **10 minutes**; turn them over and bake for **10 minutes more, 20 minutes** in all. Serve with your favorite dipping sauce. You can even eat them cold the next day as a snack.

Serves 4-6

Turkey Meatloaf

TURKEY MEATLOAF

This recipe makes a great family dinner. And if you have any leftovers, it makes a great sandwich the next day. Put a thin slice of cold meat loaf on toast, add lettuce and mayo and pack it in your **lunch box**.

"Who doesn't love a good ole' meatloaf! This dish is not only feeding your body, but also your soul. It is just perfect with fresh veggies, and my favorite BBQ sauce."

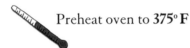 Preheat oven to **375° F**

1 ½ lbs. ground turkey	**1 egg, slightly beaten**
½ grated carrot	**½ teaspoon** garlic powder
½ grated zucchini	**½ teaspoon** rubbed sage
½ onion, chopped fine	**½ teaspoon** dried thyme
⅓ cup of your favorite healthy barbecue sauce	**½ teaspoon** sea salt
⅓ cup whole wheat bread crumbs	**¼ teaspoon black pepper**

Put all ingredients in one big bowl and mix well with a spoon or **SQUISH** and **smash** with your clean hands.

Spray or grease a loaf pan, put meat loaf mixture into the pan and smooth it with the back of your spoon. Bake in the oven for **45 -50 minutes**. Let stand for **10 minutes** before slicing and serving.

༜ Serves 6

SHEPHERD'S PIE

This is not a dessert pie; it's a *savory* pie perfect for serving the whole family for dinner. Shepherd's Pie has been around a long time and is mostly associated with England, Ireland and Scotland. The **CRUST** is made from mashed potatoes.

"I love this savory pie. The potato crust is a really cool factor of this pie. It is super yummy, I could eat this any time of year."

 Preheat oven to **375° F**

4 large Russet potatoes, **peeled and cut in quarters**	**2 tablespoons** Tamari soy sauce
3 tablespoons butter	**½ teaspoon** garlic powder
½ cup milk	**1 tablespoon fresh chopped** parsley
Salt **and pepper to taste**	**½ teaspoon** rubbed sage
¼ cup olive oil	**¼ teaspoon fresh (or dried) chopped** rosemary
1 medium onion, chopped	**½ teaspoon** dried thyme
1 cup chopped tomatoes	**Salt and** pepper **to taste**
1 pound ground chicken	**1 cup grated** cheese **(White Cheddar or Gruyere)**

Begin by making the mashed potatoes. Put the potatoes into a pot, cover with water and boil them until tender, about **15 minutes**. Drain them into a colander, and then return them to the pot and mash with the butter and milk until creamy. Add salt and pepper and set aside.

Next, in a skillet, saute the onion until softened. Stir in the tomatoes and continue sautéing over medium heat. Add the ground chicken and all the seasonings and cook for a **few minutes** more.

Put the ground chicken mixture into the bottom of a greased casserole dish. *Spoon* the mashed potatoes evenly on top and cover generously with the grated cheese. Place in the oven and **bake** for **30 minutes**, until the pie is thoroughly hot and the cheese is melted and slightly browned.

✿ Serves 6-8

NANCY'S BROILED FISH FILLETS

This is such an **easy** way to prepare your favorite fish fillets. I like to use this method for salmon, halibut and orange roughy. Don't be afraid to try something **new**. Visit the fresh fish counter at your favorite *market* and see what's available in the region where you live. On a conservation note, the Monterey Bay Aquarium has a Seafood Watch program that lets you know which fish is over-farmed and which is s a f e or unsafe for you and your family to eat. You can visit their website at montereybayaquarium.org to get current information and make smart choices.

"I love fish, so when it is paired with ginger and maple syrup...I'm in love. The unique flavor combinations are fabulous and taste amazing."

Preheat oven to Broil (about **500° F**)*

For every pound of fish, you will need:

Juice of 1 lemon or lime
1 teaspoon olive oil
1 teaspoon Tamari soy sauce
Sprinkling of garlic powder
1 teaspoon fresh grated ginger root
1 teaspoon pure maple syrup
Sprinkling of fresh ground black pepper

🐚 **1 lb. of fish serves 2**

Place fish fillet on a sheet of aluminum foil on broiler tray and turn up the edges of the foil. Pour the lemon juice over the fish, D R I Z Z L E with the olive oil, Tamari and maple syrup. *Sprinkle* with garlic powder and the grated ginger root and black pepper.

Place under the broiler (be careful it's extremely **hot!**) and broil for about **10 minutes** or until the fish is cooked through. It is not necessary to turn the fish over.

*If you've never used a broiler before, as an adult to t e a c h you how.

BAKED ZITI

All of my Italian friends have told me that Baked Ziti was one of their favorite childhood dishes. I know why. And you'll know too after you give this recipe a *whirl*.

"So cheesy and creamy. This is one of my favorite Italian dishes."

 Preheat oven to **450° F**

8 ounces ziti or other short whole grain pasta
1 cup part-skim ricotta cheese
1 large egg, lightly beaten
¾ cup finely grated Parmesan cheese
1 cup shredded mozzarella cheese
Salt and fresh ground pepper
Tomato sauce (about 3 ½ cups)

Bring a large pot of salted water to a boil. Cook pasta until al dente, according to package instructions. Then **drain** and put aside.

In a small bowl, combine ricotta, egg, ¼ cup Parmesan, and half the mozzarella; **season** with salt and pepper.

In the bottom of a shallow 2-quart casserole dish, spread half the tomato sauce. **Top** with ziti, then ricotta mixture and remaining sauce. *Sprinkle* with remaining ½ cup Parmesan and remaining mozzarella. Place casserole on a rimmed baking sheet, and bake until top is browned and sauce is bubbling, about **20 to 25 minutes**.

VEGETARIAN CHILI

So many people have asked me for my vegetarian chili recipe over the years that I just had to include it in this book. It has a lot of ingredients, but that's what makes it SPECIAL. It requires a lot of chopping and stirring, but it's still easy to make and it's the perfect thing to serve at a sleepover or party.

"You don't need meat to make an awesome chili. I love this dish due to the veggie overload. It is so yummy, filled with such fresh flavors and super nutritious."

2 tablespoons olive oil	1 teaspoon dried oregano
2 tablespoons butter	1 tablespoon chili powder
2 medium onions, chopped	1 tablespoon Worcestershire sauce
4 cloves garlic, minced	1 tablespoon Tamari soy sauce
3 stalks celery, diced	1 cup corn kernels (fresh, canned or frozen)
1 red bell pepper, chopped	1 cup cooked kidney beans (27 oz. can, drained)
3 medium size carrots, diced	1 cup cooked black beans (27 oz. can, drained)
1 can (28 oz.) diced tomatoes	1 cup cooked pinto beans (14 oz. can, drained)
1 cup tomato sauce	¼ cup chopped fresh cilantro
1 teaspoon ground cumin	Salt & black pepper to taste

Toppings:

Sliced green onions, sour cream **and/or grated** Cheddar cheese

Begin by using a large, heavy-bottomed stockpot. When butter is melted and oil heated, sauté the onions and garlic until softened. **Stir** in celery and continue sautéing. Next add the bell pepper and sauté until peppers are soft. Add the carrots and continue sautéing.

Next add in the diced tomatoes and tomato sauce. Stir in ground cumin, oregano, chili powder, Worcestershire sauce and Tamari soy sauce. **COVER** with a lid, lower the heat and simmer for a **10 minutes**, stirring occasionally.

Finally, add the remaining ingredients (corn and beans) and continue cooking for about **10 minutes**, allowing all ingredients to blend. Stir in the cilantro and add salt and pepper if needed. Vegetarian chili goes great with Blue Cornbread (page 74).

❧ Serves 8 or more

How to chop an onion*:

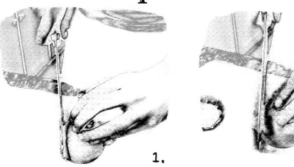

1.
Cut off knobby ends on both sides

2.

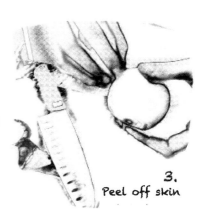

3.
Peel off skin

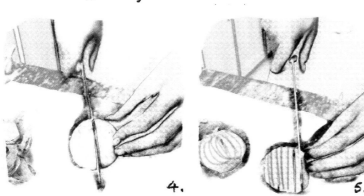

4.
Cut in half with the grain.
Mind your fingers!

5.
Lay flat and slice against
the grain into semi-circles

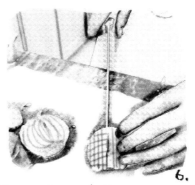

6.
Turn onion and slice across again,
creating a criss-cross pattern

*If onions make you cry, you can always wear goggles while chopping.

CURRIED SHRIMP LETTUCE WRAPS

"Lettuce wraps are fun to prepare for parties, especially when you want to serve something that doesn't require a knife and fork to eat. The Jamaican curry powder really makes these wraps something special and is a nod to my Jamaican roots."

Haile's Recipe

Seasoning Blend Ingredients:
1 teaspoon ground corriander
1 teaspoon lemon pepper seasoning
1 teaspoon Jamaican curry powder

2 fresh limes, **juiced**
1 pound fresh tiger shrimp, **peeled, deveined and cut in bite-sized pieces**

1 pint cherry tomatoes
3 tablespoons grape-seed oil
2 cloves garlic
1 small red onion
1 handful fresh cilantro
1 head butter lettuce, **cored and divided into leaves**

In a medium bowl, combine seasonings with lime juice. Add the shrimp and let *MARINATE*, covered, in refrigerator for **15 minutes**. In another bowl mix the cherry tomatoes and avocado, add juice of one lemon and set aside.

In a medium skillet, *heat* grape seed oil over medium-high heat. Add red onions and garlic and SAUTÉ, stirring occasionally, for 3 minutes. Add seasoned shrimp and cook **4-5 minutes** or until shrimp are fully cooked and pink. Stir in green onions and cilantro and remove from the stove.

Divide lettuce into leaves. Spoon about 1/4 cup of the shrimp mixture into the center of **1 lettuce** leaf. Add a spoonful of the tomato/avocado mixture to each. Fold up and over the filling and dig in.

❧ Serves 4

SULTAN'S SURPRISE

How's this for a **surprise**? A Supernatural cookbook with a recipe for one of your favorite foods...pizza! This recipe offers a healthy whole wheat pita bread crust, with fresh tomato and basil to make it especially delicious. And what's a pizza without a *gooey* cheese topping? It's a quick, easy and satisfying creation that you can top with grilled vegetables if you'd like it to be a little more colorful and robust.

"I love this pizza; it is so simple. It's packed with simple flavors that any kid will love."

Preheat oven to **375° F**

4 whole-wheat pita breads
4 medium size tomatoes, sliced
Fresh basil **leaves, chopped**
Vegetable salt, like Spike
1 pound mozzarella cheese, **grated**

Place pita breads on a large cookie sheet. Put sliced tomatoes and basil on each piece of bread and SPRINKLE with vegetable salt.

Divide cheese evenly and sprinkle over each pizza. Bake pizzas in the oven for about **15 minute**s or until the cheese is really melted. Serve right away.

🍎 **Serves 4**

POUTINE WITH MUSHROOM GRAVY

Poutine with Mushroom Gravy

* A bonus recipe from the upcoming Supernatural Kids International Cookbook. You'll have such fun cooking favorite foods from around the globe!

Poutine is a very popular French-Canadian snack food which sounds a little gross--French fries with gravy and cheese curds. In fact, the word poutine is slang for "a MUSHY mess." I decided to try to make a healthy, truly *delicious* version. Try it. I think you will like it. It's a dish that makes everyone go back for seconds.

 Preheat oven to **375° F**

1 1/2 **pounds** baby potatoes, **quartered**
5 **tablespoons** olive oil
1 1/2 **cups** broth
3 **tablespoons** flour
1 **cup chopped** mushrooms **(any variety or a mixture)**
1/2 onion, **chopped finely**
1/2 **cup** sharp cheddar, **grated**
2 **tablespoons** chives, **minced**

Place the cut potatoes in a bowl and coat them with a tablespoon of the olive oil. Place them on a baking sheet and roast them for **20-25 minutes**. You can flip them at least once while they are roasting, to make sure they get crispy. Crispy is what we are going for here.

In a little mixing bowl or measuring cup MIX 1/2 cup of broth with the flour until smooth. Set aside.

Put the rest of the olive oil into a skillet and heat it. Stir in the onion and sauté about **3 minutes**, until soft. Then add the chopped mushrooms and continue sautéing about **8 minutes** more. Next stir in 1 cup of broth and cook for **8-10 minutes** so it reduces.

Finally add the reserved broth/flour mixture and cook for **1-3 minutes** more stirring constantly to remove any lumps.

Cover the crispy potatoes with the grated cheese and pop back in the oven for **5 minutes** until cheese is melted. Remove from the oven, sprinkle with the chives and serve with the gravy.

Serves 6

Stressed spelled backwards is desserts. Coincidence? I think not!

APPLE BUCKLE

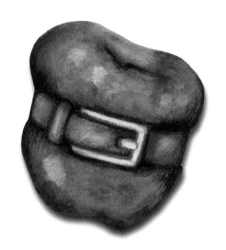

A buckle is a variation of a cobbler and it is a traditional American dish. It was often eaten for breakfast by the early colonists using whatever fresh fruit or *berries* were in season. With the fruit on the top it has a "buckled" appearance when it is baked.

Preheat oven to **325° F**

¾ **cup butter, room temperature**	¼ **teaspoon** salt
1 cup raw sugar	¼ **teaspoon nutmeg**
2 eggs	⅓ **cup** milk **(low-fat is fine)**
1 teaspoon vanilla	**3 organic** Granny Smith apples**, peeled and**
1 tablespoon grated lemon zest	**sliced**
1 ½ cups white whole wheat flour	**2 tablespoons brown sugar**
1 teaspoon baking powder	**1 teaspoon** cinnamon

GREASE an 8-inch square baking pan with butter and then dust with flour and set aside.
In the bowl of your electric mixer CREAM the butter and sugar together until smooth, at least 3 minutes. Stir in the eggs, one at a time, and continue beating. Then add the vanilla and lemon zest.

In another bowl, **mix** the dry ingredients (flour, baking powder, salt and nutmeg) together. Slowly blend in half of flour mixture into the butter mixture. Add the milk and finally the remaining flour mixture and mix until a smooth batter is formed.

Scrape the batter into the baking pan and then lay the apple slices on top. If you do this neatly your cake will look better. *Sprinkle* the apples with the brown sugar and cinnamon and bake in the oven for **60 minutes,** or until a knife inserted into the center comes out clean.

FRESH PINEAPPLE UPSIDE DOWN CAKE

This has to be one of my favorite desserts. It's especially wonderful made with fresh pineapple, though you can also use canned, unsweetened pineapple rings in a pinch. Whenever I go to Hawaii, I look for the *organic*, white pineapple that is grown in volcanic soil. They are so SWEET, so fresh and so delicious I eat a whole pineapple by myself. Really!

"There is nothing better than fresh pineapples and cake. It is such a delightful dessert, although I don't recommend eating it a lot. But every once in a while is perfect."

Preheat oven to **350° F**

4 tablespoons butter **(¼ cup)**
¾ cup packed dark brown sugar
2 cups fresh sliced pineapple, about 1 whole medium size pineapple

Batter:	**½ cup** butter**, softened**
1 ½ cups white whole wheat flour **or unbleached** all purpose flour	**1 cup** raw sugar
1 teaspoon baking powder	**1 teaspoon** vanilla extract
¼ teaspoon salt	2 eggs
	½ cup milk

Melt the butter in your 10-inch cast iron skillet. (I told you it was my favorite piece of kitchen equipment). Stir in the brown sugar and continue *stirring* over a medium heat until the mixture looks like caramel sauce. Remove from the heat and allow to COOL.

When cool, lay the pineapple slices neatly on top of the butter/brown sugar mixture and set aside for the moment.

Sift flour, baking powder and salt into a bowl. Set aside. Using your electric mixer, *cream* the softened butter and raw sugar together. Add the vanilla and blend again. You might have to stop the mixer a few times and use your rubber spatula to scrape down the sides of the bowl to make sure everything is well blended in. Then add the eggs, one at a time and blend again.

Next add half of the flour mixture. Blend and *scrape*. Then add half of the milk and blend and scrape again. Then add the rest of the flour. Blend and scrape. Finally add the remainder of the milk and blend and scrape.

SPOON this beautiful, fluffy batter over the pineapple and bake in the oven for **45-50 minutes** or until the top is golden and when you insert a toothpick into it, the toothpick comes out clean.

Allow the cake to cool and now comes the really fun part. Run a knife around the edge of the skillet. Then you turn the skillet upside down and onto a platter. This does take some practice. It might be a good **idea** to have an adult help you the first time. When you see how beautiful this cake looks and then taste it, you will be super *proud* of yourself.

❦ **Serves 8**

How to cut a pineapple:

1. First cut off both ends of the pineapple.

2. Then stand the pineapple up and cut down the sides to remove the peel, including the little eyes.

3. Next cut the pineapple into quarters and cut out the hard core.

4. Slice the pineapple into 1/4 inch slices.

BAKED BANANAS

Baked bananas are my favorite *easy* dessert. You have to try them to know how delicious they are. They can be served with yogurt, whipped cream, a scoop of vanilla ice cream or just on their own. If you like bananas, you will love them baked.

"Who knew baking bananas could be this GOOD! Sweet, zesty and unique. Yummy!"

 Preheat oven to **350° F**

¼ cup (½ stick) melted butter **(I use my microwave to melt the butter.)**
1 teaspoon grated lemon zest
3 tablespoons lemon juice
5 firm ripe bananas
5 tablespoons brown sugar

Pour melted butter into a baking dish (8-inch square). Add the lemon zest and lemon juice and stir to blend. Peel the bananas and line them up in the baking dish, turning them over so all of the bananas are coated with the butter mixture. Sprinkle brown sugar on top and place in the oven for **10 minutes.** Remove the pan and carefully turn over each banana. Then return the pan to the oven and bake for **10 minutes more.**

That's it! ENJOY!

APPLES UNDER

This fruit crumble has to be one of my favorite **DESSERTS**. You can fancy it up with whipped cream or your favorite ice cream or just eat it on its own like I do. And it's so *easy* to make.

"Apples and cinnamon are the best together. Stick em in the oven and you get sticky, yummy and spiced up apples."

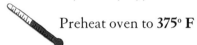 Preheat oven to **375° F**

5-6 cooking apples **(like Granny Smith), peeled, cored and sliced**	Crumb Topping:
2 tablespoons raw sugar	**1 cup** rolled oats
½ teaspoon cinnamon	**½ cup** whole wheat flour
¼ teaspoon nutmeg	**1 cup brown sugar**
Juice of 1 lemon	**½ teaspoon** salt
	½ cup (1 stick) cold butter**, cut in small pieces**

It's easier to peel the apples if you leave them whole. Then you have something to hold on to. When peeled, CUT the apples into quarters, cut out the core and slice them. Place apple slices into a bowl, add the sugar, cinnamon, nutmeg and lemon juice and mix around with your clean hands. Butter a 2-quart baking dish and layer the apples in it.

 In another bowl mix the oats, whole wheat flour, brown sugar and salt. Then add the butter in small pieces. This is especially fun to **mix** with your hands, making sure the butter is well blended into the oat mixture. The mixture is supposed to look *crumbly*. Place the crumble mixture over the apples and bake in the oven for **50-60 minutes**, until the fruit is *bubbling* and the top is golden brown.

✁ Serves 6

PUMPKIN BUNDT CAKE WITH WHITE CHOCOLATE & PECANS

This is one delicious cake—moist, spicy and sure to please everyone. It's made with canned pumpkin so you don't have to wait until the holidays to make it. It's a little known fact that there is more beta-carotene (a very important nutrient) in pumpkin when it is cooked. Like many **orange vegetables**, pumpkin is loaded with vitamins and minerals as well as fiber. You can give a SPOON of it to your dogs too since it's also really good for them.

The hardest part of this recipe is GREASING and flouring the bundt pan but once you get the hang of it you'll be able to do it in no time at all.

 Preheat oven to **350° F**

3 cups whole wheat flour **or white whole wheat flour**	**1 ¼ cups** vegetable oil
2 teaspoons baking powder	**1 teaspoon** vanilla extract
2 teaspoons baking soda	**One 15 ounce can of** pumpkin
3 teaspoons cinnamon	**(approx. 2 cups cooked, mashed pumpkin)**
1 teaspoon salt	**1 cup** white chocolate chips
4 eggs, beaten	**½ cup** chopped pecans **or walnuts**
2 cups raw sugar	

BUTTER and flour a bundt pan. Use a little bit of paper towel and soft butter to do the job and try not to miss anything on the sides or in the middle of the pan.

The next step is to put a little flour in the pan and kind of **swoosh** it around until there is a dusting of flour everywhere. Like the butter, you don't want to miss a spot with the flour. Giving the pan a hard SHAKE will loosen all the excess flour so you can dump that bit out. (It should only be a little because we don't want to waste anything we don't have to). Set the pan aside.

Sift all the dry ingredients together into a big bowl. I put everything through the sifter—the flour, baking powder and soda, spices and salt. Mix with a wooden spoon and set aside.

In another bowl or in your mixer, **beat** the eggs and sugar together until they look light and creamy. Add the oil and pumpkin and continue beating at medium speed. Now slowly stir in the flour mixture, a bit at a time. Finally FOLD in the chips and the nuts.

POUR the batter into the bundt pan and bake in the oven for **60 minutes.** I use a long skewer (kind of like an extra long toothpick) to test the cake to make sure it's done. Let the cake sit for at least **30 minutes** before you turn it upside down onto a cake platter. Bundt pans are heavy so you might need some help doing this the first time.

Wait about half an hour more before you dig into your masterpiece.

CHINESE CHEWS

This recipe was POPULAR when I was a kid. Everyone liked them and I baked this **sweet treat** often. I don't know why they are called "Chinese Chews" because there is nothing Chinese about them. No one really seems to know. I guess it will always remain a **mystery**.

"I love these chews! The nutty sweetness is just the perfect treat."

Preheat oven to **350° F**

1 ½ cups whole-wheat flour	**4 eggs, beaten**
1 cup raw sugar	**1 teaspoon** vanilla extract
2 teaspoons baking powder	**2 cups chopped** pitted dates
½ teaspoon salt	**2 cups chopped** walnuts

In a mixing bowl or in the bowl of your electric mixer, stir the flour, sugar, baking powder and salt together. Next add the *beaten* eggs and vanilla. Finally stir in the dates and the nuts.

Spread the mixture out in a greased or sprayed baking pan (about 14 Inches x 9 inches x 3 inches). Put in the oven and   for 20-25 minutes. Allow to cool, then cut into bars.

1. Vanilla Plantifolia - flower

2. drawing of the vanilla bean from the florentine codex c. 1580

BLUEBERRY PEACH QUINOA CRUMBLE

"I prepared this tasty dessert with the help of Chelsea Clinton on The Rachael Ray Show. Yes, it's fun to cook with a President's daughter and it's just as much fun to cook with your family and friends. Think of your kitchen as a playground, a place where you can create healthy foods that are palate pleasing as well. I'm a big fan of quinoa and this crumble gives you another way to enjoy it."

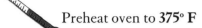 Preheat oven to **375° F**

1 dozen medium peaches
1 cup fresh blueberries
½ cup cane sugar
2 teaspoons cinnamon
⅓ cup almond meal flour
1 tablespoon cornstarch
Nonstick cooking spray

For the Crumble:
1 cup light brown sugar
1 cup almond meal
1 cup quinoa, rinsed
1 ½ tablespoon cinnamon
⅓ cup flax seeds, ground
½ teaspoon nutmeg
1 cup coarsely ground almonds
1 cup room temperature butter,
    cut in chunks

Haile's
Recipe

Peel and slice peaches; add to large bowl with the blueberries. SIFT sugar, cinnamon, almond meal and cornstarch over the fruit and mix together.

Lightly *spray* a 9x13 pan with nonstick cooking spray. Place the fruit mixture into the pan. In another large bowl, mix together all crumble ingredients except the butter. Add the butter and mix together with your hands. The mixture will begin to come together but still crumbly.

Top the fruit with this mixture, lightly mixing in a little bit as well. Bake for **45-55 minutes**. Top will be golden, fruit will be BUBBLING.

Cakes, Cookies & Desserts

Simply the Best Brownies

SIMPLY THE BEST BROWNIES

For all the chocolate lovers in the world, and there are many of us, this is a **simple**, wonderful recipe guaranteed to *delight* everyone.

"Who doesn't love brownies? These are truly, 'simply the best' kind of brownies."

 Preheat oven to **325° F**

½ **cup** butter
2 **ounces unsweetened** baking chocolate
1 **cup** raw sugar
2 **eggs**, beaten
1 **teaspoon** vanilla extract
1 **cup chopped walnuts (optional)**
¼ **cup whole wheat pastry flour or** white whole wheat flour

Melt the butter and chocolate together in a saucepan over low heat, stirring constantly with a wooden spoon. When melted, remove the saucepan from the heat and stir in the sugar. Next add the eggs and vanilla and stir until *smooth*. If you are using nuts, add them now. Stir in the flour and blend well. This batter will be thick.

GREASE an 8 inch by 8 inch baking pan with butter. Line the pan with parchment paper, then grease the paper. Pour the batter into the baking pan and spread evenly. Bake for **40-45 minutes**, or until a toothpick inserted into the center comes out clean. Let the brownies cool a bit before cutting and serving. Double **YUM!**

PEANUT BUTTER & CHEDDAR DOG TREATS

I live with two dogs, Buddha and Ringo. I wanted to create something special and healthy for them because they like snacks just as much as we do. These treats are **fun** to make. And shouldn't a Supernatural Kid have a Supernatural Dog?

 Preheat oven to **300° F**

1 cup milk (use low-fat if your pooch is a little on the chubby side)	**½ cup** oat bran
½ cup natural peanut butter **(the smooth, not crunchy kind)**	**1 cup grated Cheddar cheese**
1 egg	**2 ¼ cups whole wheat flour**
½ cup wheat germ	

Pour milk and peanut butter into the bowl of your electric mixer and blend. Next add the egg and continue blending. Add the wheat germ, oat bran and Cheddar cheese. When mixed well, slowly add the flour until it forms a dough.

Roll the dough into a ball and place it on a lightly floured surface. Using your rolling pin, **ROLL** out the dough until you have a circle, about ¼ **inch thick**. Use your favorite cookie cutter to cut into SHAPES. (Mine are heart-shaped because I love my dogs very, very much.) There will be dough left when after you cut the shapes, so put the dough back together and roll out again, until you have used all the dough.

Place the biscuits on a greased baking sheet and bake for **30-40 minutes** until they are lightly browned on top. These biscuits should be CRUNCHY. Allow to cool, and then store them in the refrigerator in an airtight container.

ACKNOWLEDGMENTS

My heartfelt gratitude goes first and foremost to Judy Proffer, who encouraged me to update my original Supernatural Cookbook and who continues to inspire and delight me every time I'm in her golden presence. No one could have a better co-conspirator or friend.

Special props go to my talented goddaughter Alexandra Conn, for her artistic contributions and for the joy she has brought to my life since the day she was born.

Also a special shout-out to my original posse of Supernatural junior chefs—Malie Miller, Anya and Kai Andrews and Arum Butler-Sloss. To all the friends who passed through my kitchen and taste-tested the recipes—you know who you are. Without all of you, life would be so dull.

I would like to thank Charmaine Thomas with all my heart for raising such an intelligent, beautiful and focused human being like Haile. Being a great mother is the most important job on the planet.

Buddha   Cisco

AWARD-WINNING BOOKS BY NANCY MEHAGIAN

Siren's Feast, An Edible Odyssey, 2008

"A spicy brew of recipes and adventures."
~ Quincy Jones

"A journey of the senses. Like Water for Chocolate…with cayenne. Lots of it."
~ Linda Gray

"Mehagian is a wonderful writer, with a capacity to bring people and places to life and have them leap off the page in waves of intense prose."
~ myinnerfrenchgirl.com

The Supernatural Kids Cookbook, 2011

"Nancy's Supernatural Kids Cookbook is inspired."
- Bridget Fonda

"The cookbook tempts eyes just as the recipes tempt palates."
~ Gail Cooke

"Long before Jamie Oliver, Oprah Winfrey, Alice Waters and First Lady Michelle espoused the virtues of healthy and mindful eating, epicurean Nancy Mehagian created a little collection of vegetarian recipes for the junior set, in an effort to inspire her then five year old daughter to develop an appetite for natural fare."
~ My Daily Find

"What better way to excite young imaginations and introduce kids to the fun of creating in the kitchen than this gorgeous cookbook from writer, healer and cook Nancy Mehagian?"
~ LA Arts Beat

EVERY KID.

HEALTHY FOOD.

EVERY DAY.

NO CHILD SHOULD GROW UP HUNGRY IN AMERICA

But one in five children struggles with hunger. Share Our Strength's No Kid Hungry campaign is ending child hunger in this nation by connecting kids in need with nutritious food and teaching families how to cook healthy, affordable meals. You can help surround kids with the healthy food they need where they live, learn and play.

Pledge to make No Kid Hungry a reality at NoKidHungry.org.

NOKID
HUNGRY®
SHARE OUR STRENGTH

CPSIA information can be obtained
at www.ICGtesting.com
Printed in the USA
LVIC06n0105131014
408439LV00003B/5

9780983812067